£9 95

March

Also by Andrew Taylor

Liverpool Warehousing Co. Ltd. (zimZalla, 2016)
Airvault (Oystercatcher, 2016)
Future Dust (Original Plus, 2015)
Radio Mast Horizon (Shearsman Books, 2013)
Comfort and Joy (Ten Pages Press, 2011)
The Lights Will Inspire You (Full of Crow Press, 2011)
The Sound of Light Aircraft (Knives Forks and Spoons Press, 2010)
The Metaphysics of a Vegetarian Supper (Differentia Press, 2009)
And the Weary Will Rest (Sunnyoutside Press, 2008)
Poetry and Skin Cream (erbacce-press, 2004 and 2007)
Temporary Residence (erbacce-press, 2007)
Cathedral Poems (Paula Brown Publishing, 2005)
Turn for Home (The Brodie Press, 2003)

Andrew Taylor

March

Shearsman Books

First published in the United Kingdom in 2017 by
Shearsman Books
50 Westons Hill Drive
Emersons Green
BRISTOL
BS16 7DF

Shearsman Books Ltd Registered Office
30–31 St. James Place, Mangotsfield, Bristol BS16 9JB
(this address not for correspondence)

www.shearsman.com

ISBN 978-1-84861-505-2

ACKNOWLEDGEMENTS

Poems have previously been published in the following publications:
*1/25, Bone Orchard, The Camel Saloon, Confingo, Establishment, em,
Mad Rush, The Merida Review, Moths at the Bus Stop, New Walk, off
With, Otoliths, Push, Raindogs, Recours au Poems, The Red Ceilings,
Question Mark, Shearsman* and *Stride*.

'Culvert' appeared in *A Festschrift for Tony Frazer*. 'Welsh Hills',
'Early Harvest', 'The Pads', 'Liverpool 11, Leeds 116¼', 'Loft Poem',
'Small Fall' 'Port Song' and 'Follow the Flock' appeared as part of the
liner notes to the CD *Last Year's Leaves: Tape Reflections Vol. 1* by My
Autumn Empire, released by Sound in Silence Records (sis026)
soundinsilencerecords.bandcamp.com

Grateful thanks to the editors.

Contents

for Rachel Smith and Nichola Taylor
and to the memory of
Keith Harrington, 1963-2014

Welsh Hills

it starts with a bell
then the harmonium

it is Sunday after all

a piano wheeled
to winter beach
before being chopped

beyond the seven miles
the seven hills

at dusk quiet river
glow aside from
the blank field

patched with darkness

get a line to London
inland the birds
are circling

from the tower share
the view from the second
floor kitchen

watch the cloud roll in

Honesty Box

This is not automatic
it has to be earned

Capturing moments of sounds
and noises before they escape
through the ceiling

In the hopes of preserving something

felt tip painted nails
I will build a shared archive

Greenness of meadow
redness of terminus lights

Early morning empty platforms
prospect of four into two
a day on the network

wait twenty years to search
for peeled paint

Foliage insulation
good for cold May

Shell collecting a rippled shore
wash the finds in pools

Follow tracks in soft sands
keep the notes
focus on the corner chair

Hold the seeds
to your face
walk The Pads

spot the scarecrows
spot the swallows

across to the city
see the cranes see the spires

there's blood there's soil
there are generations

Old School free range eggs
honesty box
pass the feather

let's always share

Empty for Depot

At the foot of the proposal bridge
the path meanders

At the second time of asking
it was agreed

despite information and the essentialness
of cable laying

during the boiling of clouds and chimney smoke
on a cold day

you arrived and secretly I knew that light
would be altered

shapes would shift along the shore
and evening platforms

would provide desired reunions before trains
return empty to the depot

Stickers on Notebooks

like clear skies
   that turn to cloud
it is necessity

dig through sand seek lines
   make camp

verge offers opportunity
   West Coast Mainline

shortening days leaf
   silhouettes against roofs

picnic near parks
   picnic in motorway service areas

Station

four tracks two fast
two slow

Island platforms
unmanned after
two p.m.

East Coast
Mainline

north to Scotland
south to London

we are
somewhere
in-between

watching leaves
twist in the
fast train
wake

Blue String

seals the bag
contents slightly
damp

they will eventually
burn

despite rain
a clear view

she played on sand
summer past

grains shift

but love stays
the same

she wants snow

to build shelters

Snow Castles

There is beauty in the steam pipe
It is somebody's magic place

a solitary walk
among distant breakers

will avoid the crescent queue

Unpack the bags carry the tree

the badge will be nestling
the coincidence of image

will startle

A Mast Year

Despite the wind
      it is impossible
to fly the kite

She runs along
      the concrete path
that's been there

forty years

Though the orchard
      is reduced to one
tree the windfalls

mount up

they will make
      a delicious pie

The kite folds neatly
      away to be stowed
until we meet

during the remnants
      of the next storm

Medium Wave

Green retreat
along the canal

berries gathered
sugar to sweeten

a starred cardigan
first play

first two added

don't let them rot on the vine

beacon of return
with it drops the mist

at junction

curve sweeps the river
follows the line
south end reflected

slightly just
enough to know

it is there

Daisy Picker

Ivel runs low
   riverside walk shade
Daisy picker
   dead leaf book marked

Culvert

for Tony Frazer

beating
in its cage
a connectivity

close curtains
on lightening

don't be afraid
to call

crows as clever
as seven year old
children

foxes guard eggs
in the coop

to seek perpetual
spring

of early mornings

Yellow Tape

Wrap the beech
in a fertiliser
bag

seal with yellow
tape

seek the artificial
leaf

an explanation
of the importance
of home

Scottish Blend

Like the plain it is probably
the water

airport lights five miles away
seem closer

green signal allows for movement
along the coast

Work to an early morning deadline
sleeping bag sleep

walk to the station
to take a five pound shower

before resumption
the rain brings out the swallows

Under Sleepers

This city is at its best
　　it is like L.A. but cooler

ship is docked against
altered skyline

those left remain adequately
poised for museums

Albion House
　　　they called the names
from the second floor balcony

on the tide she leaves
stow the gear

put the kettle on

Sun Tint Glazing Gap

for Cliff Yates

Only ever hours away
from the cutting tunnels

through sandstone

Follow line of canal weeds angle flow

salmon and blue striped top girl
bobbed hair looks like a Belle and Sebastian
cover star

at lunch we time it just right

hand painted billboards coach station
look and feel of airport departures

bridges narrow cut narrows
we turn at the basin

After Coke at Ikon John Salt
Gallery Two bump into Rob

talk about Scott and Sarah's wedding

on departure angle
of fields hedgerow divides
sun tint glazing gap

Mist House

Solitary cut
adrift

headlights into
eyes

half light
twin lanes

hedgerow curve
revelation of
mist house

lit from within
like
an
artwork

First Wings

Snow gathered
red cross green arrow

like the toll booth
approach at midnight

it encloses drops
like a trickster

salt clears route
floodlights deflect
columns a permanent

light

beyond production
logistics warehousing

its thickened air paths
of ghosts lead forward

spooks suddenly

a roadside cat

The Hum

Shape from somewhere
leads
nowhere

depthless

conceals foundation

angled uniformly

solidity

the hum
of electricity

Smoke Whispers

Krysta exhales
it's a whisper
like sudden mist
from the lake
it eventually fades

There are Holiday Homes

During the week
    there is nobody

a dead area

it *looks like a desert*
in *the middle of the forest*

Security of mist
    destination or shelter

there is no lit window

can Ambien wake
    the near dead?

depth of silence
    virgin snow

cello song breaks
    piano chord repeats

masks footfall

Frozen Servants

Slow motion
alone
voices distant
a silence
deflected
by
mist

Diamond Tea

This is not 1990
    this is 2012

land permissions   cooling tower
cloud cover

take it easy with the drugs

"Where's Sean?"

"He'll be laying on his back looking at the stars"

from beyond
    message continuing support

take it easy with the drugs

This is April it is not May

there is an epicness about this
    like a ten pence valentine
yet to be sent

refuge of fire
    out there beyond
the river
    bound homeward

5.15 a.m. record the sound of bird song
    and motorway
from the security of the service area

blanket wrapped couple
    bonfire stare

throw another pallet on

Duracell is breathing fire
      Ringo is asking the same question
over and over and over

Easter
      often cloudy

every Preston Guild it will snow

paint splattered Dolomite

not even 25.6 mg can warm

this is April it is not May

Teresa Ran out of Tape

Half light   over points
power drain milligram fade

you join as a choir
     like flour added to an enamel
bowl
you expand

painted nails   white
kick the heel

left   right
just in case

share morning coffee spot
out at the bay

I have the t shirt

Blue Bitter Proud

the south   is not the north
first class trace
air-conditioned sunshine
alcohol return

kick the heel smash the cowbell
through Suzie's lights

match machine

Bikini beach
     record overlook

slow formed breakers
morning…

Sleep   back of the bus milky sun
                across abandoned pools parks shacks
     everything is quiet

stillness of empty spaces and forgotten stretches of land

  kids scream out the lyrics
          No black light thank you

UK once again armed with puffy coats and NyQuil

Drugged up smiling ear to ear

It was utterly nourishing to connect with someone else

It was insanely beautiful

The air was warm
          over the city
pieces of feathery down floated like soft snow

swirling in the wind
          nudging feet and calves.

she feels high

Hope it lasts
the deepest winter awaits us
we'll see how it goes…

[acknowledgements to Morgan Kibby]

Poem for Morgan Kibby

Rows to themselves
pretty empty flight
Warsaw was cancelled

wedge the white wine
in the snow to chill

take portraits
of the first ladies

through the warmth
there is the smell
of tired creaky bones

after flu in the cold
tired mornings

nobody there for
a simple hug

The ferry crossings
offer respite
meadows of ocean ice

some drank wine
on the sun deck
it was peaceful

misty upon departure

the church an unexpected
safe haven was full
of love

Coffee and Flowers

Scent carries
            in winter

it is almost interchangeable

remaining leaves
            gathered

await disposal

to add a layer
to
tarmac

Smitten

From the cottage window wild deer
roamed paused took a look at the honeymoon couple
concerned with keeping warm

Isolation of the finest kind morning
          leads to evening
slow paced   like The Lilac Time
spending summer playing tennis

rescued from routine excitement
loss purged
she appears fresh from Italy with desire
and the knack of making coffee
a rescue act   from the decimation of parted angels

she made him believe in the stars once more

city-centre hotel the turn of the millennium
the river slate coloured   tidal

she watches gardening programmes
and eats room service

a warm welcome after returning from
the hip party
through Mathew Street's madness

the room looks like a shoot from *Vogue*

Like Nina

Red coat and flats
        like Nina it's the eyes
green hint of light

crackle of points
like solo piano

rid the organiser
of clutter
        ignore foreign language
eat salad

move lavender paper
its role is defined

like tunnel fluorescents
        it is combined
with necessity and emptiness

bundles of rags
        dockside wait to be shipped

follow the wake

four minutes between
        descent it's
like the Fens I imagine
field recordings

pastoral urban
        within covers

within conversation
    she is called
beautiful

Tell Me of the Boulevards

Regardless of quality
make the fold

the tabloid in half

write messages to the dead
they may answer

Satellites store unused numbers
tape recordings oxidise

most days I'm tied to the north

Clear the ditches of growth
it's easier to jump

Look for strands of something
to give a clue

Like tulips leaning towards the light
it pays to seek

Plated Echo

Paris never
sounded so good

Carry of cable
    underground

a capture

Dust dampened
movement restricts

Weather forces
    indoors

consideration

like simple mortar
we are prone

to crumble

We Demand the Sun

Place the rosemary
into the rain

We hope you will
be happy
in your new home

Green through
cold colours
of late spring

Birdhouse
camouflaged
against Victorian
brick

Herb garden
umbrella canopy
the blue shed door

gap a latent afternoon
refuge

Neek

A coldness
large and white
like a Russian Winter

It's the gap
that does it
the wait

for a new elusive
ideal summer

the thermometer
doesn't show it
the calendar does

such vulnerability
a transient work
this will not
sort your head out

take the window seat
it is actually a pew

with the selling
of the gold
there was talk
of security

but there never was
security

Elizabeth on the Sofa

The hope to age
together from youth

Forward with blessing
influence beyond years

since enforced silence

like candle wax on oak
it is hard to remove

Extra Shot

It's as if
she's still here

you can buy
that smell
in any pharmacy

Booths removed
relegated to a lower
league

Dan's boots
are ten years old

'Good morning
would you like
your coffee any
stronger?'

Beautiful patterns
made by
the rain

She thinks
it may flood

Nivalis

for Simon Scott

non-stop
        falling snow
visual flow
          no intentions
to venture outside

write until the snow stops
  take
two days

clear ice from the doorstep

heater flat
out
push
the temperature
up

season change
  noticeable
in north Liverpool

Shipping

You have to get above the air
to properly taste the lemon

engineering brick used by Victorians
when drilled reveals the ancientness

of dust

Like the logistics of sending books
to Hollywood

track the movement

that summer was both the greatest
and most tragic of his life

get absorbed into the details

Eleven people in a room
their silence contained

There is 139 calories in each original tube

Contingence

for Nils Frahm

Compress sound
                dampened

layer the felt

noise keep less familiar

sound piano actions

                accidents become
                        music

*as we left Berlin there was
a blizzard*
                magic

kind pause
                sustain

Shp-shp

        Ffrrr

Ctt Ctt

everybody needs a moment

[with thanks to Lauren Strain]

Twig Bucket

A preference for industrial architecture
   store cupboard Saturday mornings
cut the cheese thinly place it in wholemeal

sometimes the cellar would flood
   when the culvert spilled

take it as a lark
                  despite being a romantic
I prefer the hedgerows prepared for
winter

she can't take her mind off the harvest
the days are getting shorter

Tall blue eyed
the stars are fading and peeling
their boldness is losing lustre

Stickers are losing their glue

the four seasons is not just a hotel

   cities polish up well when the sun shines

make the edit crisp
     jump without looking down
it will only frighten you
black tipped nails offer few clues
     perhaps the dented middle finger

will

tear the fence down
burn it throughout autumn and winter

Drinking coffee
out of paper cups with plastic lids

The lemons are from Turkey
                          container enters
motorway corridor

pace gather a sense of runway

strip light replacement
                          across point ghost tunnel

river gradient
glow of ink shine of ink

condensation on the inside of a plastic lid

underground

take the technical work it through

there is the possibility of a rainbow

first encounter
                  river view

Tom would take the commuter ferry
in early evening mist

wait! the office is not yet open
by chance the cup is brewing

pilgrimage seven streets expanded
views from the floor

neon of Exchange Bar reflection
        leaves tambourine tumble

knee high boots weather
accordion stops
                tail end of hurricane
or is it a severe storm

between March and December
                        annual communication

carve your useless names
                before the storm gods
unleash

here they are!

don't wear corduroy before your time
keep paper cuts clean
make sure not to slag people off in poems

you will be plagiarised

Don't drink Gin in the winter

the young won't get it the young won't get it
tell us what you want and tell us what you need

Listening to Scott Walker
                loudly
it really should be played
in a rented house in Bootle
on Mordaunt Shorts

reading a big paper

\# 66 but the bottle is #12131

The fence has been cut
                it burns with a crack
sparks rise like bubbles in a vintage glass

the blanket is for coverage
stay with it buddy boy!

run to the grocery
unless you want frozen pizza

I'll fix you some coffee

Oh we're all out of it
you had rather a lot last night

Lent Shift

for Rory Waterman and Libby Peake

Bloodaxe tags exit Sheffield
architecture provides roost

*like when a man isn't allowed booze
or crisps and he shrinks*

it is easier to tunnel than climb
through the valley remaining snow
dry stone remote clipped hedge borders

like when a fox sniffs around
the wheelbarrow that has lost a wheel

Out here the electricity looks different
gathered against loose walls

Slowly climb tracks find their own way
pylons accept the gradient

Like a solitary hare in a field of spring shoots
that has strayed from safety

the nearer to the sea the clouds gather pace
the bells will ring between 1.30 pm and 3.30 pm
for Sunday services half muffled for Lent

depart repeat follow the lines to the Square
announcement along Station Street
past hordes of tricky trees

There's not an ounce of feather

like a partly demolished outhouse there is internal
growth that proves that decay favours form

Quiet Zone

There'd be enough fuel for two winters
the route over the bridge is mossed

hint of sapling beyond the leafless sycamore

soon the heavy rivers will flood

From this vantage point
the curvature is apparent

Maundy Thursday

Wake me when this is over
clear the snow lifeless leaves

the path is tiled
years of footsteps

lent lily
goose leek
get indoors
regardless of associations

allow for your head to bow
at will Spring tonic slake
the thirst of midnight

the palette yellow of morning

cracked egg breakfast
though the wood
ignites with persuasion

the provision makes for
occupation garage shelter

look to the beams the stuffing
will release upon tearing

Network

WEST KIRBY Beach walks office home [10.36]

HOYLAKE Angela Keaton organic bad curry paste

MANOR ROAD Hotel pick up Rooney's goal against Arsenal

MEOLS Red frame white light rose bush bridge

MORETON Defunct brickworks production shed

LEASOWE Typhoo garden goat

BIDSTON Borderlands line

BIRKENHEAD NORTH Change go back on yourself *just at the Penguins x*

WALLASEY VILLAGE skirt the moss under the M53 bamboo screen

WALLASEY GROVE ROAD double bridge poppies among the weeds

NEW BRIGHTON the cliff rock points cable ariel light aircraft ships at sea lawn patch repair kit perfume counter smell late foxgloves

WALLASEY GROVE ROAD double bridge poppies among the weeds trackside fire

WALLASEY VILLAGE skirt the moss under the M53 bamboo screen
Stuck at Wallasey Village trackside fire between Grove Road and the power is off :-(

Oh! At the station or just stuck in the middle of nowhere?!
Stuck at station think I'll have to find a bus or something :-(
You going to give up or make it back to Liverpool and beyond?
All the other lines are working so will try to get to town perhaps or
Birkenhead
Ah ok. Keep me posted!
Will do
Running again:-)
Sorted quickly then hey?!

BIRKENHEAD NORTH Change go back on yourself

CONWAY PARK above light concrete

HAMILTON SQUARE please mind the gap when leaving the
train

JAMES STREET cleanliness of white but for how long?

MOORFIELDS a thousand or more journeys

SANDHILLS docks oil rig platform sailing

BANKHALL burnt out pub

BOOTLE ORIEL ROAD Hugh Baird College view to the
north docks

BOOTLE NEW STRAND tower blocks star of the sea

SEAFORTH and LITHERLAND scrapyard wide platform

WATERLOO interchange

BLUNDELLSANDS and CROSBY David Lydiate's LightNight
image girl with butterfly tattoos trackside workers

SEAFORTH and LITHERLAND scrapyard wide platform

BOOTLE NEW STRAND tower blocks star of the sea

BOOTLE ORIEL ROAD Hugh Baird College view to the north docks

BANKHALL burnt out pub

SANDHILLS docks warehouses peninsula

MOORFIELDS 15 minutes

LIME STREET closed

LIVERPOOL CENTRAL under

JAMES STREET the removal of the Mersey Bookstall

HAMILTON SQUARE few passages

BIRKENHEAD CENTRAL curve of tunnel curve of exit new edge

GREEN LANE no electric light do not alight here rise

ROCK FERRY follow the line of the river

BEBINGTON RSK

PORT SUNLIGHT soap

SPITAL meeting place twenty years apart

BROMBOROUGH RAKE banks of ferns

EASTHAM RAKE automatic doors

HOOTON bunting a decoration no need to change welfare pod

CAPENHURST licences nuclear site they've altered the lane

BACHE green of canal green of fields disused platform

CHESTER quiet lines slow approach allotment sheds depot shade Royal Mail the whistle of departure immediacy of departure [14.27]

Three Blue Hours

the icon flashes blue
it is due to start

two plays in it is engrained

how does a voice
sound like that?

From the first
at three lanes
to the July greens

Avrocar perfect
a moonlike beach

solitary
it appears
skirts rare clumps of green

like it knows

Two Summers

Spread across through idents
re-recorded
it's always the first impression
that embeds

gather little rocks underfoot
four buoys out
return with souvenirs
to wash

in the breakfast sink

knowing of travel
where are the tea chests?

Beat the heat wave into submission
exit early exit late

use selection wisely watch it loop
there must be lag

like walking into path wide webs
at dusk

Wash Dry Fold Now!

Winter ready
long walks   short days

the slope will
become treacherous

as the oranges are brought home

Heat the milk   blanket at the ready

despite condensation
WriteRoom   four a.m.

silence broken wrens dart

[acknowledgments to Jonah Bromwick]

Minster

Just the right edge
of cold once
the mist has left

spring sun sequence
in order stained glass
reflection

on ancient markers

Brass on oak
permanence carved

let's leave a reminder
of illuminated mosaic

Three Blanket Season

Struggle not to look
it's touching
take time to halt it

fire cracking floating
star in resin
truthful yet frightening

some details don't lie

Emilie donates her flats
Maddy skips along the dock

the letter its anonymity
causes aura

could you be winter?
hidden behind books

the dull life in checked shirt
bobble on the wrist

Passing Place

Stonechats dart before the prow
down five miles of single track

ten year atlas
                      fifty year old map

John Bartholomew & Son Ltd Duncan St Edinburgh

Along the burn a diversion
slow flow   fast flow

Mary's Bridge becalmed
stone gathered clear pool

shaped like the original
pool of home

Freighter

Journeys that follow
old routes
invisible mapped
by satellites

freight box carried
through zones

buy the organic
and gold top milk
skipping early
co-ordination

lanes lead directly
to paths near rivers
charted walked

patch of grass temporary
camp quickly
assembled picnic

the place to which
to return

Saturday Before

under engineer boot
chippings shift

new window wrapping
temporarily glued

Behind five hours final time sharing sun

Stop look listen

yellow rise steel current
on rail

watcher's position
towel across sill

Bible or remote close at hand
concrete sleepers remain

Mending Kit

Enter sit

a line written in the shelter
square marked territory

And gaze

And gaze

leaves gathered framed
straw lined diagonal

at the sky

at the sky

Open
summer until 17.00
winter until 16.00

Early Harvest

Don't let the wheat waste
sackcloth lifts on motorway bridge

a spider runs across a pillow
in a suburban bedroom

let's take a walk through
stalked fields

track the wires trace wide tyre tracks

it must be time soon for
the swallows to return

were they the ones arcing when we left
quickly to beat the storm?

new shelves in the lychgate
moss on the old wood
replaced lintel over the door

sandstone shelters
border the footpath

ten bantam eggs £1-00 a festival candidate
walk the circuit route two days running

second solo dodging rain

The Pads

Undulate
        hidden
until gathering

like stairs to the poetry room

it is use

perhaps a hint of decay

Captured
          considered
despite rain

that repeats
a motif on roof glass

hours later

Liverpool 11 Leeds 116¼

for Matt Fallaize

They've covered the path in tarmac
I prefer the traceability of steps

follow the curve seek the culvert
beyond ditches the 57 strums along

a solitary swift
one of the few left in this part of the world
struck by curve and grace
the elegant lines of its wings

a tinge of sadness
a couple of weeks ago
the swift would have had a dozen
or more companions
but slowly
they disappear

there's an air of melancholy
attached to the final swifts of the year
like the last Test match of summer

each spring piercing shrill shrieks
a harbinger of longer days softer air

on cue as they start to leave
the wind gets up the showers grow more chill
the air becomes fresh

watch seasons roll in and out
behind their tail-feathers

few birds look at home as the swift
the briefly visiting symbol of our fugitive summer

until next year then

Loft Poem

at home here

a 'Chaos' painting
propped
rolled canvas

empty crates
against
full cases

at this time
the air cools

the light fades
and the eyes tire

slight coating
on glass

it may be time
to pull the blind

and close the hatch

Pacing Call

Like glass in a turned field
it is recognition of shift

I prefer Tarmac in re-laid
car parks at twilight

with the evening calls of birds
the sharing of information

becomes priority

Small Fall

Up amongst the eaves
the typical time in minutes

Wrap the pastry in plastic
then in its paper bag

Walk the slower route
through earlier tracks

Butter the freshly cut bread
replace the underfelt

You know it's September
when the robin appears

Shirt sleeves lowering sun
yellow fourth buoy visible

small fall of leaves
Ben's acoustic guitar

a fitting farewell
to the Island

Port Song

Fade out
   a green to amber

the bricks are made with
Mapperley clay

Pacific inference
   strings and machines

Click of a hotplate designed
to keep freshly brewed coffee warm

three conkers
   gathered for sill

Work with what is available
allow the outside inside

a healthy way
   to disappear

Mick sings of fog on the waves
and a world up for auction sale

Stillness light
   through gaps

Follow the Flock

across shorn fields
   a gathering
brook banks cleared

roll of clouds
   boil across
hedge colour burst

young green stems
   cut through
incline slight gradient

sandstone core lane
   true edgeland
gentle sweep back

The Rainbow

Wood takes two
and a half hours

Paper is product

small talk
        over ravioli

battery holds its charge

I've seen how
        she looks at you

It's how I look at her

fingers leave marks
there will be DNA

should the rains fall
we will be protected

Midland corridor
calm window
        motorway curve
split
track takes me to you

Strike on the plate not on the granite

Gutter remnants
    reflector
warmth of tobacco
warehouse
    scent of bale

Rust on points
    in black stride
waiting room
platform
    year long bloom

mortar gives way
    to angled growth
tunnel Victorian brick
gateway
    arched canopy

16 minutes north
    2 degrees colder
the walk begins
itself
    a provider

Go, Take in the Beauty

stand to the right
keep hold of the handrail

on the last night in San Francisco
we missed The Album Leaf

red lights through terminus fence
the rails can and do lead to you

wear the battery down it can always
be charged

power through points that sound
cold it is better to leave to return

There is a wind within dreams
falling from the sun

through summer fog stand still
until we are the last

Lightning Source UK Ltd.
Milton Keynes UK
UKOW01f1123130917
309109UK00001B/69/P